Capturing Creativity

20 Easy Ways to Bring Low-Tech STEAM into Your Classroom

by

Melissa Unger & Anna V. Blake

ISBN: 978-1-387-26057-7

This book is dedicated to:
John E. Blake, beloved father of Anna V. Blake
1944 - 2021

and

The Pittsburgh Education Community—we couldn't have
made this book without your influence!

With Special Thanks to Remake Learning and the
Allegheny Intermediate Unit for the support and ability to
make our dream a reality.

A Note on How To Use This Book

When we wrote this book, we envisioned that this text would be a resource for educators to help infuse STEAM learning into any classroom. As we talked with colleagues in the Pittsburgh education community, we realized that this project could serve multiple purposes, and thus, we wanted to help show the ways this book can be useful to educators, parents, and those in higher education.

As an *educator*, we envision that you can use our book as a resource to bring new STEAM activities into your elementary classroom. Using our one-page activity guides and accompanying instructional videos, you can easily gather the materials and follow step-by-step instructions to get started. Our greatest hope is that STEAM will be taught in every classroom, and this book helps that dream become a reality.

As a *parent*, we wanted this book to be a guide that provides low-tech STEAM activities for any household. Each activity uses common materials found at home. With this in mind, we felt these activities could be fun on a weekend, or especially in the summer months when school is out. Using the QR codes and accompanying YouTube videos for each activity, we hoped that your family can bond over completing STEAM activities together.

As a *student or professor in higher education,* we believe that this book can serve as a topic of discussion and influence for the Maker Movement in elementary education. We both wished we had a book like this to help guide creative student teaching lessons or even to write a paper on why STEAM education is so important for young minds. Reading the words of many educators will provide insight into the teaching profession and will hopefully influence how the next generation of educators will enter the classroom.

Table of Contents

Prologue
The Maker Movement

Dr. Jeffrey Evancho & Peter S. Wardrip

Agency by Design Pittsburgh

Humans have been learning since the beginning of their existence, whether it be through trial and error, problem-solving or simply trying to understand things that are out of our conceptual reach. Making things has always been connected to our respective cultures where we made our clothes, our tools, our furniture, and our meals. As we learned what it meant to be a part of our culture and our communities, we learned this through *making*, observing what was made, and talking about it. We know that when we make things visual—that is quite literally MAKE things—human sensemaking is being facilitated and in turn, learning in general is compounded.

Throughout history, making has defined certain moments in time, such as the Renaissance and the Industrial Revolution. In the last 15-20 years, a maker movement has emerged. The Maker Movement finds itself at the intersection of exponential technological growth and the resurgence of arts and crafts. As an educational movement, Making values the need for learning to be hands-on, interdisciplinary, and holistically situated during a time of interconnected local and global challenges.

Pittsburgh, Pennsylvania, has emerged as a champion of the Maker Movement, sparked by its local contexts creating the opportunity for the movement to take off. Perhaps it is the industrial heritage of the city that makes the city comfortable to support Makers. The current maker movement in Pittsburgh has been the convergence of several factors. The city's philanthropic leaders have been prescient in their support of making for youth learning (see remakelearning.org, for example). The school districts in Western Pennsylvania have been experimental and creative in encouraging their students and teachers to engage in maker-based learning experiences. The museums have been national leaders in the design and assessment of learning through Making (for example, makingandlearning.org or makinginmuseums.org).

In 2012, a group of researchers from Harvard's Graduate School of Education began a research project to better understand how to support learning through Making. The project was titled Agency by Design (see agencybydesign.org). The project is primarily named after the conceptual framework of when people make things, they develop personal agency, and that agency can in turn empower them to use their new learning in ways that benefit self-motivations. Agency by Design has a core framework that maps the key outcomes of Making as *Looking Closely*, *Exploring Complexity*, and *Finding Opportunity*. When these sensibilities are developed through the making process, we gain agency in our new learning and understandings.

The research project partnered with educators in Pittsburgh to engage in this work. Over time, the project culminated in a book (*Maker-Centered Learning: Empowering Young People to Shape Their Worlds*, Clapp et al., 2016) as well as thinking routines. However, the project continued and evolved. Now Agency by Design Pittsburgh (AbD PGH) annually has a cohort of educators from the region. They work together to be more intentional in how they support student learning and engagement through Making. The authors and contributors of this book are leaders in that community.

Today, AbD PGH is a research practice partnership designed to connect educators from diverse maker-based learning environments for the purpose of developing mutual understandings of maker-centered learning and assessment. Specifically, the teachers come together in the community to address their need to assess and document learning in maker-based experiences. AbD PGH typically consists of 30 educators from 20 different organizations (school and out-of-school environments) annually and within Western Pennsylvania. These educators work with learners from grades PreK to 12. As the community has evolved, while student agency is still paramount, AbD PGH has also developed a focus on values-based assessment. Through this focus, educators are supported to:

- Identify what they value for student learning and engagement;
- Articulate what it looks like for students to engage in that value;
- Design learning experiences that elicit evidence of student learning and engagement in that value

The community frames "values," as the kind of learning and engagement that they feel is important in their classrooms and ultimately contributes to what they want their students to be beyond school. The values that AbD PGH members have identified include curiosity, collaboration, problem solving, persistence, and creativity.

We are excited for the release of *Capturing Creativity: 20 Easy Ways to Bring Low-Tech STEAM into Your Classroom.* While these educators are sharing ambitious and creative learning experiences, they are also demonstrating their intentions for the kind of learning they hope to design. These educators represent a diversity of learning goals, tools, and materials that guide their design. As the area of Maker Education develops further, we should all be so lucky to have resources such as this to share ideas, but also exemplify intentional design for the learning and engagement that each of us value.

*Dr. **Jeffrey Evancho** is the Director of Partnerships and Equity, Northgate School District.*

*Peter S. **Wardrip** is an Assistant Professor of STEAM Education, University of Wisconsin-Madison*

Memorable Making Experiences

Melissa Unger & Anna V. Blake

Authors

Think back to a time when you made something that you were really proud of. Maybe this was a new recipe that you made with a special family member, or a volcano for a science fair in sixth grade. You have that memory in your mind, don't you? You remember this experience like it happened yesterday. What details do you remember from this experience? Why do you think it was so significant to you?

For many of us, making something new evokes a sense of pride and teaches us more about ourselves. As educators, we want to bring that sense of pride—sense of *agency*—to our students. As we reflect on our own experiences as Makers, we hope that this text leads you to some reflection of you own.

For Melissa, Making was a form of self-expression. In middle school, she began designing and writing her own monthly magazine called *Peoples Bulletin & Journal* (PB&J for short!), which she then distributed to family and friends.

Inspired by an idea from a popular cartoon, Melissa quickly found herself absorbed in coming up with ideas for articles, interviewing people, and writing reviews of restaurants, movies, and more. What started as a few paragraphs on a piece of paper, evolved into 20-30 pages per issue. Decades later, Melissa still feels like this experience helped to shape her into the person she is today. The confidence that came from sharing her work each month with others helped her to develop her love of writing and gave her an outlet to think creatively. Now as a teacher, Melissa works to encourage her students' creativity and challenges them to pursue their interests to see what they can discover about themselves.

For Anna, Making as a child was a way to escape. Being dyslexic, Anna did not excel at reading or math in elementary school, but instead, enjoyed the creative STEAM projects that her fifth grade teacher Mrs. McCleary created. From writing a play about colonial America to creating a booth at a colonial fair, Anna discovered that fifth grade was the most fun year—due largely to these experiences. Later in her schooling, Anna encountered another STEAM teacher, Ms. Walker, who had her sixth grade science class build volcanos, make a diagram of the phases of the moon, and many other hands-on activities. These projects inspired Anna to keep challenging herself in all of her subjects. Without these Making experiences, Anna does not feel that she would have been as engaged in school. Making allowed her to explore and build up her confidence in academic skills. In her current role as a computational thinking and computer science teacher, she works with many students who remind her of herself in elementary school. By introducing Making to students, Anna believes that she is inspiring the next generation of learners.

With these two vignettes, we wanted to share how Making and creating something new can impact students in different ways. However, bringing hands-on learning into the classroom takes work and we must examine this central question: *How do we create quality, low-tech, high-impact STEAM and Maker learning experiences for all students?* Use this question to guide your reading of this book as you start to bring low-tech, high-impact STEAM activities into your teaching practice. This book is a collection of interviews and contributions from creative, innovative, STEAM-focused educators in the Pittsburgh education community.

When schools in Pennsylvania shut down in March, 2020, and transitioned to virtual learning because of the COVID-19 pandemic, Melissa and Anna began to ponder how to keep the momentum going for STEAM learning. After discussing the issue, an idea was born: *What if teachers from around the region could create and share virtual STEAM activities that could be used by all students?* The Pittsburgh STEAM Station quickly emerged and continues to thrive online at YouTube.com. Through the writing, planning, and making of each episode, Melissa and Anna found that more and more teachers wanted to be involved. In all, 26 educators from 19 school districts took part in 34 episodes.

With thousands of views, The Pittsburgh STEAM Station became a resource for both teachers and students to discover fun and engaging STEAM activities. Melissa and Anna watched with excitement as other organizations, teachers, and students used The Pittsburgh STEAM Station to learn and engage throughout the 2020-2021 school year. One such instance happened in Spring, 2021 at Greenock Elementary School in Elizabeth, Pennsylvania. Teachers organized an all-day STEAM event for students using nine activities from The Pittsburgh STEAM Station. Each child started the day with a bag of materials, which included string, paper, straws, and more. Students went from classroom to classroom learning a new STEAM concept with each teacher. Activities included building a boat, making a paper airplane, creating a parachute, and developing a marble maze. Teachers had the option to play the accompanying STEAM Station video and give students time to build, or to show the students a demonstration and give them the opportunity to watch the video at home from a QR code. The day was a success and many students had extra materials to take home and continue learning during the summer months. This is just one example of how low-tech, high-impact STEAM can be brought into a school to engage students.

As you read through this book, you will find material lists and QR codes that will take you to each episode of The Pittsburgh STEAM Station. Activities are organized by topic and various educators provide insight that will help you imagine how you can bring STEAM into your classroom. Keep in mind your own memorable Making experiences and think about how you can bring the same joy, curiosity, and excitement to your students.

We encourage you to look at The Pittsburgh STEAM Station on YouTube.com and also to reach out to us with any questions.

Enjoy!

Follow us on *Twitter* for
additional STEAM resources:
@MelissaUnger15
@AnnaVBlake

Chapter 1
Building a Foundation

"Man's mind, once stretched by a new idea, never regains its original dimensions."
Oliver Wendell Holmes

Introducing STEAM projects into your classroom can seem like a daunting task at first, but for educator **Kristy Frohliger**, STEAM became a natural extension to her science and social studies curriculum.

"I am now a dedicated STEAM teacher," Frohliger explained. "But prior to my current role, I taught both fifth grade and a Gifted class. I've always spent considerable time examining my curriculum and identifying how I can make topics more exciting for students."

As a fifth-grade teacher, Frohliger initially began introducing her students to STEAM learning by designating every Thursday as a STEAM day. "During these sessions, I would provide students with a hands-on STEAM project that reinforced a concept related to what we were working on throughout that week."

Over time, Frohliger's students came to look forward to each Thursday STEAM session and she started to notice a greater sense of engagement among her students, as well as less absenteeism on those days. Additionally, Frohliger most appreciated the high-level reflections and responses that students provided after each project. "For me, one of the most critical aspects of a strong STEAM challenge is the opportunity for reflection at the end. Reflection is most definitely a skill that students have to work on throughout the process, but by giving them the chance to debrief on what they learned, what worked well, and what they might do differently next time, I see a huge increase in students' ability to problem-solve and think creatively," Frohliger said.

However, STEAM projects can be difficult, Frohliger cautions, until students learn to work together as a team. "Collaboration is a huge component of STEAM learning, and it is something that students really need to work on. Often students' first reaction is to complain that someone is *copying* off them when they share a similar idea. One thing that I try to instill in every student is that they can use each other as a resource—can learn *from each other*," said Frohliger.

When first starting with STEAM in your classroom, Frohliger has a few suggestions:

First, consider gathering easy-to-find, low- and no-cost supplies. Collecting recyclables, cardboard boxes, interesting-shaped containers, and craft materials can go a long way in building up a stock of useful building materials.

Frohliger sends out a list of requested supplies to her school community and uses bins in her classroom to keep materials organized as they come in. Dollar stores, craft stores, and online sites such as Amazon are also a great way to purchase low-cost materials in bulk. Many items can be ordered from dollar stores by the case, often making them even cheaper than one dollar each.

Frohliger's second piece of advice is to pair STEAM projects with literature. While books focused on specific academic concepts are great for providing students with concrete examples of STEAM in action, books that focus on problem-solving, perseverance, and collaboration help students learn the social-emotional skills that come from engaging with STEAM learning.

Finally, Frohliger also recommends focusing on trends: "One of my favorite things about teaching STEAM is that it is very much focused on real-world experiences. Many of the projects and challenges that I do with my students highlight current events and popular technology because that is something that is relevant now. I often look to what is impacting my students at this point in time—it could be anything—a particular game that students are interested in, programming and robotics, issues with the environment.... I try to craft lessons around the topics that make students' learning feel most relevant to them."

"When you teach the curriculum through STEAM, you show students how what they are learning in school relates to the outside world. Even simple projects using materials like paper and recyclables can give students a deeper understanding of how topics can be applied to real-world concepts," said Frohliger. Frohliger's telescope activity (p. 51) and helicopter challenge (p. 53) both show

how low-tech projects with simple materials can help capture students' interests and spark their imaginations.

Reflection Questions

Frohliger highly recommends having students engage in reflection after each STEAM activity. Whether students are discussing their thoughts with their peers or writing them down on paper, it is important to give students the opportunity to think not only about the task they just completed, but also about the thinking, problem-solving, and perseverance that went into it.

- What surprised you about this challenge?
- What was an idea that you tried, but then found out it would not work? What did you do instead?
- How did you collaborate with your teammates?
- What frustrated you about this challenge?
- What was something that you did that worked really well? Why?
- How does what you did in this project apply to real life?
- What would you do differently if you were to try this challenge again?

Tallest Tower

For this challenge, use materials that you have around you to create the tallest possible tower. Your tower must stand on its own and not fall over when you let go of it!

Scan to access related STEAM Station episode!

Materials:
- Blocks or anything stackable!

Step #1: Gather materials and construct your tower. Think about what materials might be best for the *base* of the tower (the bottom), and what might be best for the top.

Step #2: After you build, measure your tower. *How tall is it?* You can use a measuring tape or ruler to measure in inches or feet or choose something else to measure with. (For example, the above tower is three cups tall!)

13

Extension Idea

Explore examples of architecture from around the world. Examine structures and compare designs.

Eifel Tower, Paris, France

Epcot, Disney World

Parthenon, Athens, Greece

City Skyline, Dubai, UAE

Encourage students to experiment with *shapes* as they build. *Are particular shapes better to build with than others? Why?*

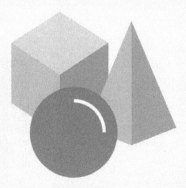

Boats

Have you ever noticed that when you put things into water, some objects sink, while other objects float? That is because of *density*. If something is more dense than water, it sinks. If it is less dense, it floats. Can you design a boat that floats and holds weight?

Scan to access related STEAM Station episode!

Materials:
- Container of Water
- Tinfoil
- Marbles or Pennies

Step #1: Form your tinfoil into the shape of a boat. The body of a ship is called its "hull" and the hull usually has curved sides and an open top.

Step #2: Gently place your boat into a container of water. Does the boat lay on the top of the water? Does water appear to be getting into the boat's hull?

Step #3: Once you are sure that your boat can float, begin adding weight. See how much weight your boat can hold. Does it matter *how* you add the weight? Should it all be added to one side of the boat, or spread out? If needed, redesign your boat. Is there a way to make your boat hold *more* weight?

Extension Idea

Explore the concept of density and determine what types of items sink and float. Gather a variety of items in different sizes, shapes, weights, and materials.

Fill a container of water and gently drop each item into the container. Prior to adding each item, make a prediction: *Will the item sink or float?*

As you test your items, see if any patterns emerge—do items of specific size, shape, or weight tend to float? What conclusions can you make about density?

Bridges

A bridge is a structure used to go over a physical obstacle—usually water, a road, or a valley. There are many types of bridges, but all use supports to help them withstand the weight of whatever needs to travel over top of them. Can you build a strong bridge?

Scan to access related STEAM Station episode!

Materials:
- Recyclables
- Cardboard
- Found Objects

Step #1: For this project, determine what materials you want to use, as well as a design idea for your bridge. A bridge is a structure that goes *over* something else. What will your bridge *go over?*

Step #2: Begin building your bridge. Consider what supplies you will use to support your bridge. What will give your bridge height?

Step #3: Add something as the surface of your bridge and then test your bridge's strength. How do you know if your bridge is sturdy?

Extension Idea

Explore the various types of bridges. How might the design of each bridge help to hold weight?

Arch Bridge
Uses an arch to transfer the weight of the bridge across all parts. These bridges become stronger as time goes on!

Cantilever Bridge
Uses *cantilevers*—horizontal structures that are supported on one end

Suspension Bridge
Suspension cables hung from above support the main platform of the bridge.

Cars

We use cars and other vehicles to get around every day. Wheels and axels help cars to move through the streets. Can you build a small car of your own?

Scan to access related STEAM Station episode!

Materials:

- Small Box
- Sticks (for axels)
- Round Objects (for wheels)

Step #1: Find a box to act as the body of your car. You may want to decorate the box with details from real cars—add windows, doors, or headlights!

Step #2: Poke four even holes into your box. There should be two holes on each side, and they should be parallel to (across from) each other.

19

Step #3: Insert axels into the holes. The axels help the wheels to spin. Once added, attached a wheel to each end of the axels.

Step #4: Test your car. Give it a push. Do the wheels help the car move? If not, make some improvements to your design.

Extension Idea

Turn this activity into a simple physics exploration of ramps, angles, and friction!

First, create a few ramps of different angles and see if you can make your car move. What happens when your car moves down a steep hill? How about a slight hill? Next, add different textured materials to your car track. Use smooth materials such as cardboard or plastic, and rougher materials such as fabric, sandpaper, or foam. Which types of materials allow your car to travel best?

Related Projects

Scan the QR codes for STEAM Station episodes.

Car Tracks

Pulleys

Cup Stacking

Educator Interview:

What is the BEST part of STEAM learning?

"I love watching the 'ah-ha' moments as students problem-solve with their classmates to overcome the challenges they face. The amazing creativity that students express and the passions they find along the way refuel my passion for education every time. Their pride of ownership in the learning is exhilarating!"

Jody Kokladas

"My favorite outcome from incorporating STEAM into our curriculum is how we are able to introduce our students to things that they may have never done before, or would not have the opportunity to do otherwise. We have something for everyone, and the level of new learning and enthusiasm is infectious."

Aaron Colf

"When students are given the opportunity to be hands-on, the creativity pours out of them. You can't stop it if you tried! My favorite student outcomes are seeing their genuine joy and engagement and the conversations that they have through STEAM learning."

Ashli Detweiler

"Experiments and STEAM activities allow for productive failure—children learn that some things just don't work and determine what went wrong to find better solutions and designs to solve problems. Students learn to be adaptable and to think like problem-solvers with a growth mindset. They learn through trial and error and have the opportunity to think critically and problem-solve on their own."

Stephanie Schultz

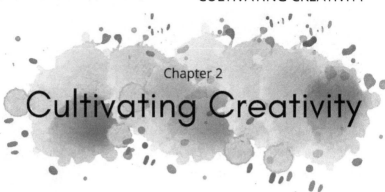

Chapter 2
Cultivating Creativity

*"Creativity now is as important in education as literacy,
and we should treat it with the same status."*
Sir Ken Robinson

For **Rachael Ragan**, an Elementary STEAM teacher who teaches students K-5, helping students to develop creative thinking skills is of the highest importance: "Something that I really pride myself on is being a creative problem-solver. That is something that has really helped me in life—not just as a Maker, as an artist, but in every aspect of life. Creative problem-solving allows you to better interact with others, have productive conversations, and look at situations from different perspectives. That is something that I want for my students, and when I am designing my curriculum, I keep that goal in mind," Ragan explained.

From the beginning of the school year, Ragan sets the tone in her classroom by giving her students creative prompts that are as open-ended as possible. "For example, one prompt that I use is to 'Make a Hat'. Whatever kind of hat that you want to make is fine. The only thing that it has to do is stay on your head. How you get it to stay on your head is a whole engineering challenge in itself; the materials that you want to use—that's design thinking. Projects like these help students get into the creative mindset," said Ragan. Additional open-ended prompts might also include "Make something to hold something," or "Design a chain reaction to complete a task." (Check out Ragan's chain reaction challenge on page 81.)

Ragan also encourages her students to start small and build on their learning: "I like to provide students with a foundation in sculptural techniques so that they have a firm understanding of how materials can be used together and how to attach them in order to get their project to *do* or to *look like* what they are imagining. We focus a lot on attachment techniques (like using tabs or flanges to help something stand, or making a brace to support a structure) so that students can move from designing in 2D to designing in 3D." Ragan recommends direct instruction at the beginning of the year as students are just learning the necessary skills, and then providing more freedom to explore their materials and their own ideas as the year progresses.

Providing examples of Ragan's own creative thought process is another way that she works to encourage her students. "I try to provide many different examples. Not necessarily of the exact project that I want them to create, because that often leads to imitation instead of creativity, but I model my thought process for coming up with an idea. I show them the materials and then talk through what I might do with them. For example, I might show students a jar and then say, 'Well, what could I do with this? It is glass, so it probably is not good for throwing, but it opens up, so it might be good for holding things. Maybe I can…'. Conversations such as these can serve as a jumping off point for students to share their own ideas," Ragan explained.

Ragan acknowledges that one of the biggest challenges for teachers in a STEAM classroom is management. With so many projects, materials, and ideas, it can be difficult to feel organized and in control. However, Ragan has a few tips to help other educators:

First, be as flexible as possible, especially if you want the students to get creative. Even if *you* have an idea about what *you* want the students to create, you need to keep an open mind and allow students the space to bring forth their own ideas. Sometimes a project will turn out completely different than what you expect, and it is important to be okay with that.

Second, limit supplies. Limiting supplies does not limit students' creativity, but instead, gives them the chance to really focus in on an idea and explore creative uses for their materials. For example, if you provide tape, skip the glue. Or, tell students that their project must incorporate exactly four different elements. By providing parameters, your stress level as a teacher will also go down, as you will know that you have all the needed materials, and you can also better ration your supplies.

Third, prep materials, but not too much. If you are working with cardboard, you will quickly find that young students have a difficult time cutting it. Ragan recommends pre-cutting materials into the correct-sized pieces, but not necessarily cutting them into specific shapes. "If you want students to make cardboard fish, for example, cut the cardboard into an appropriate size, but then let students cut out the actual shape of the fish. This will help students accomplish the task, but you will still get a diverse set of projects. They will not be as 'cookie-cutter' as they would be if you cut out all the fish yourself," Ragan explained. You may also want to look into collecting chipboard or cereal boxes for students to use.

When Ragan reflects on what she wants her students to get out of STEAM class, it is not a specific project or a specific content that she wants them to remember; rather, it is a mindset: "I want students to be able to look at different materials and not just see them as a piece of cardboard, or a ball, and instead, be able to think about what they can do with those materials, what they can make. I want my students to develop an 'Artist Outlook' where they are constantly thinking about and imagining what they will create next."

Attachment Techniques

Ragan starts her school year by making sure students have a strong foundation in building skills so that they can use their skills to create increasingly more intricate projects throughout the year. Below are some of the attachment techniques she teaches her students.

- Flange
- Tabs
- Brass Fasteners

Optical Illusions

An *optical illusion* is when something tricks your eye into "seeing" something that is not really there. One type of optical illusion is called a **THAUMATROPE**—*an illusion that takes two images and makes them look like they are combined into one.*

Scan to access related STEAM Station episode!

Materials:

- Paper
- Pencil
- Tape & Scissors
- Markers

Step #1: Cut two small squares of paper, about 3 inches each and create two separate drawings that when blended together, will create a picture. (Examples: Bird & Nest, Frog & Lily pad, Spider & Web)

Step #2: Color your images. (Bold colors work best for this activity.)

Step #3: Tape your squares to the pencil, so that the pencil is in between both squares.

Step #4: Hold the pencil in your hands and rub your hands back and forth so that the pencil spins. Look at your squares. Are the images blending together?

Extension Idea

Scientists study optical illusions to better understand how our eyes and brain work together so that we can see. In order to identify an object, our brain separates it from its background. Different people may see this object differently, depending on what their brain chooses to "see" as the background!

Take a look at this image. Is it a vase or two faces?

Flipbooks

A flipbook is another form of Optical Illusion. By flipping the pages of a book really fast, the images will start to look like they are moving. By creating similar images with slight changes on every page, you will be able to create your own *animation*—a moving picture!

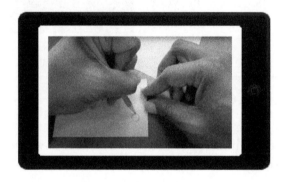

Scan to access related STEAM Station episode!

Materials:
- Sticky Notes or a small stack of Paper
- Binder Clip
- Pencil

Step #1: Decide on a topic for your flipbook. Draw an object on the first page of the paper. (Tip: Easy animations to start with are a bouncing ball, rocket, or shooting star.)

31

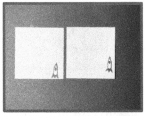

Step #2: On the second page, draw the same object, but in a slightly different position. Keep going until you have many pages.

Step #3: Attach the binder clip to your papers to keep them all together. Then, flip through the pages quickly to see if your image looks like it is moving. What else might you add to your animation?

Extension Idea

Now that you have created a simple animation, use your understanding of a how a flipbook works to create your own story.

You may want to start by designing a *storyboard*—a graphic organizer that helps you to plan what will happen.

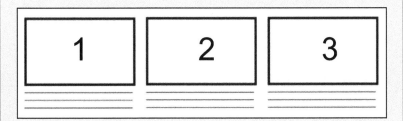

What will happen first? Second? Third? How will your characters move or change throughout the story? Sketch out your plan before creating your flipbook.

Popup Cards

Sending and receiving cards is a great way to communicate with others, and in this challenge, you can explore working with both two-dimensional and three-dimensional shapes as you create your message.

Scan to access related STEAM Station episode!

Materials:
- Paper
- Scissors & Glue
- Markers

Step #1: First, create the base of your card. Fold your paper in half and create a crease.

Step #2: With the crease toward your body, create two cuts in your paper, about 2 inches apart.

Step #3: Fold the cut backward and then open your card. This should create a three-dimensional box.

Step #4: Add shapes, colors, and designs to your popup card by gluing pieces onto the paper and share it with someone special!

Extension Idea

After creating a popup card, experiment with combining multiple 3D shapes into your very own popup book! Can you use 3D images to convey a story?

Shadow Art

Have you ever stepped outside on a sunny day and noticed your shadow? Shadows are made by blocking light, so when you stand outside in the sun, your body blocks the sunlight and casts a shadow on the ground below. See if you can create your own shadow art!

Scan to access related STEAM Station episode!

Materials:
- Toys or different shapes
- Sidewalk Chalk
- Pencil & Paper
- Flashlight (optional)

Step #1: Choose a variety of interesting toys and shapes. Place them on the sidewalk on a sunny day and look at their shadows.

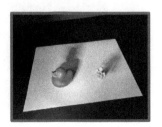

Step #2: Using sidewalk chalk or a sheet of paper under your objects, trace their shadows and turn your drawing into a work of art!

Cloudy day? This activity can also be done inside by working in a dark room and using a flashlight to shine a light on your items.

Challenge: Create a shadow art drawing at different times of the day. What do you notice? Do the shadows outside change size throughout the day? What do you think is happening?

Extension Idea

Shadow puppets have been around for over one thousand years and were once a popular way to tell a story. Can you create your own shadow puppets using dark paper? Create an image, cut it out, and attach it to a stick so that you can hold it. Then, turn out the lights, grab a flashlight and shine it on your puppet. Does the puppet cast a shadow on the wall?

Related Projects

Scan the QR codes for STEAM Station episodes.

Origami

Paper Caterpillars

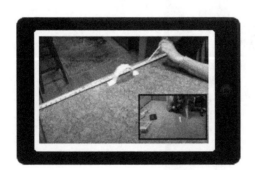 

Color Trick

Educator Interview:

What is your top tip for integrating STEAM into your practice?

"Just start! I think a lot of teachers say they don't know where to start when it comes to STEAM—just gather a handful of materials and let kids explore. You can find a STEAM lesson for lots of concepts in your curriculum. A quick Google search or look on Pinterest is a great way to find ideas!"

Stephanie Schultz

"You cannot have control over every aspect of the project. Allow it to take on its own path and give students a chance to share and ask questions of each other!"

Colleen Hinrichsen

"Survey the students! Our kids have wonderful minds and are extremely thoughtful. Survey the students to explore their ideas on how to connect content to real life. This will engage and empower them to take ownership and the application will have deep meaning that will result in an enriching learning experience."

Lisa & Crosby Tiberio

"Reach out to families, businesses, local colleges, and retired teachers for assistance, whether financial or volunteering. Have students donate recycled items such as Lunchables and Danimal containers. Ask Walmart's photo center to keep film tubes, Bath & Body Works to save candle packaging, small coffee shops to save pastry cardboard boxes, and family members to keep toilet tissue and paper towel tubes."

Michelle Wiltrout-Sparrow

Chapter 3
Embracing Curiosity

"A mind that opens to a new idea never returns to its original size."
Albert Einstein

A lifelong Maker, **Stan Strzempek** jumped at the opportunity to develop a MakerSpace at his school. "When I think about my own education in elementary school, it was the hands-on activities that really stick with me all these years later," Strzempek recalled.

With a focus on active engagement, his MakerSpace (known as the Collaboratory), gives students the opportunity to interact with their grade-level curriculum in a way that provokes curiosity and a sensitivity to detail. For example, when first grade students were learning about pollination in their science class, Strzempek planned a visit with a local beekeeper and then a flower dissection lab so that students could better understand the process.

"I like to keep the following advice in mind: Keep things fun. Build on background knowledge. Connect the dots. Be exciting," Strzempak explained. By designing projects that further bring classroom concepts to life, students are able to make deeper connections to real-world topics.

Having a dedicated space for STEAM learning has been an important component to helping students become more excited about science. "The Collaboratory has created a positive space that kids want to visit. Because the room is central in the school, students 'window shop' as they walk by. They are curious about what is happening inside and are excited to learn when they get there. Students who normally struggle in a traditional learning environment, thrive alongside their peers in the Collaboratory," Strzempek said.

The collaborative nature of Strzempak's class often gives students the chance to not only develop academic skills, but also to practice working together as a team, and helping each other out. The MakerSpace works to boost students' social and emotional learning by providing plenty of opportunities for collaboration.

Nature and physical science have played a huge role in Strzempek's teaching experience, as prior to his time in the Collaboratory, he was a science teacher in a special education high school setting. "Teaching the sciences really makes you focus on systems and how things work," Strzempek said.

This attention to systems helps Strzepek plan his lessons. "Collaboratory projects revolve around themes. Students are given all the tools and background knowledge they need before they are presented with a problem. Their job is to come up with a solution. Lessons are focused on *process* instead of product, which gives students the freedom to make choices," he explained.

By focusing more on *how* students go about their tasks, rather than focusing on their successful completion, students start to see that it is not always about getting the correct answer, but instead, about thinking critically and using their creativity.

In order to help students focus on the *process* of their work, Strzempak uses the Engineering Design Process (EDP) to break down each step of a project. He begins by encouraging students to ask questions and he defines the constraints of the task. Then, students must brainstorm before making a plan and collecting materials. Next, students create their project or complete their task, and then they share their work and consider possible improvements. When using the EDP, there is a focus on iteration and creating multiple solutions.

Outside of the classroom, Strzempek enjoys spending much of his free time outdoors, whether it is mountain biking, hiking, or simply spending time in nature. "So often, my teaching ideas come to me while I am just going about my day. I tend to be inspired most when I am out in nature because there is just so much there to capture your imagination."

Many times, projects that he brings to his students use simple materials such as recyclables to focus on sustainability. Strzempek's parachute design challenge (p. 45) and bubble wand activity (p. 47) both use commonly found items. "What is neat, is seeing how students take a challenge and run with it. I like to see how their own creativity comes through as they are working," Strzempek said.

Strzempek offers the following advice to other educators interested in starting a MakerSpace and helping their students develop their sense of curiosity: "First, choose an event, an object, or a place, and then create a challenge, a problem, or a question relating to it. Next, make things fun, meaningful, and personal. Think about the students you are designing the learning experience for. What do you want them to get out of the experience? Praise students for dreaming big, failing forward, and risk-taking. And finally, create opportunities that promote collaboration and self-discovery."

Strzempek's passion for inspiring students and instilling in them the power of curiosity defines his teaching style. "I am always looking for ways to help students develop their curiosity. Curiosity can take you anywhere."

Looking Closely

As a member of Agency by Design Pittsburgh (see *Prologue*), Strzempek regularly uses AbD thinking routines to guide his practice and help students cultivate their curiosity.

Throughout any Maker experience, it is important for students to gain an understanding of the complexities and the systems at work in their designs and prototypes. When encouraging students to look closely and think critically, Strzempek recommends that you:

- Have students generate lists of parts, things they notice, or connections they can make to other topics
- Encourage students to ask questions of themselves and their peers
- Give students the opportunity to try to make sense of a problem or explain a topic in their own words

(see agencybydesign.org)

Parachutes

A parachute is a device that helps to slow the motion of something as it falls through the air. Can you build a parachute that will help a toy land safely on the ground?

Scan to access related STEAM Station episode!

Materials:
- Paper Cup
- String
- Plastic Bag or piece of Fabric
- Scissors
- Small Toy

Step #1: Poke four holes in the top of your cup using scissors. This will become the base of your parachute.

Step #2: Cut four pieces of string, all the same length. Tie one piece of string to each hole.

Step #3: Tie your strings to the corners of the piece of fabric or attach them to the handles on the plastic bag.

Step #4: Place your small toy into the cup and drop your parachute from a high location. Watch it fall to the ground. Does it fall slowly? What else might you add to your design in order to increase the time that it takes to fall?

Extension Idea

If you throw something up into the air, it is going to eventually fall back down. That is because *gravity* pulls objects toward Earth. However, parachutes work by creating *air resistance*—parachutes push back on the air around them to slow your fall.

Experiment with different types of materials for your parachute.
- What happens if you use a small piece of cloth?
- Or a large garbage bag?
- Can you make a parachute out of a piece of paper?
- What about out of a piece of wood?
- Does the type and size of the material matter?

Bubble Wands

Bubbles are a mixture of soap, water, and air. When water gets trapped between layers of soap, a bubble forms. Can you design a bubble wand that helps you to blow your own bubbles?

Scan to access related STEAM Station episode!

Materials:
- Pipe Cleaners
- Container of Water
- Dish Soap
- Spoon

Step #1: Use your pipe cleaners to create various shapes. Bend the pipe cleaners into circles, squares, triangles, and more.

Step #2: Attach handles onto your pipe cleaner shapes so that you will be able to easily dip them into bubble solution.

Step #3: While you can use pre-made bubble solution if you have it available, you may want to try making bubble solution of your own. To do this, mix together 1 cup of water with ¼ cup of dish soap. Once created, test your bubble wands!

If the bubble solution is too thin, add more soap. If it is too thick, add more water.

Extension Idea

Using your bubble wand, test out some of these challenges. Make observations. What do you notice about your bubbles?

Can you:
- Blow a large bubble?
- Blow a small bubble?
- Blow a bubble inside a bubble?
- Stack bubbles?
- Poke a bubble without popping it?
- Make a bubble land in your hand?
- Change a bubble's shape?

Waterslides

Waterslides are always fun on a hot day! These slides use ramps and water to help you move quickly from the top to the bottom. Can you design a mini waterslide?

Scan to access related STEAM Station episode!

Materials:

- Recyclables
- Cardboard
- Tinfoil or Plastic Wrap
- Small Toys

Step #1: For this project, determine what materials you want to use, as well as a design idea for your waterslide. In order for something to move down a slide, the slide must be set up as a ramp.

Step #2: Build your waterslide using cardboard and recyclables. Consider lining your waterslide with tinfoil or plastic wrap so that the cardboard does not get wet.

Step #3: Test your waterslide. Place a small toy at the top of the slide and pour water down the slide. Is the toy able to move? What might you change about your design to improve the waterslide?

Extension Idea

How might what you created as a waterslide help to inspire an idea for a rollercoaster? A rollercoaster uses steep curves and big hills to create a fast-paced, fun experience for riders. If you were to design your own rollercoaster, what would it look like?

Telescopes

Think like an explorer! Telescopes are special tools used to make distant objects appear closer. While actual telescopes use lenses or curved mirrors, this simple project allows you to build something that will help you focus in on an object and look closely!

Scan to access related STEAM Station episode!

Materials:
- Paper Towel Roll
- Paper or Plastic Cup
- Tape & Scissors
- Markers

Step #1: Cut a hole in the bottom of your cup. (Use caution if cutting a plastic cup with scissors!)

Step #2: Push the top of the paper towel roll through the bottom of the cup and attach it with tape.

Step #3: Decorate your telescope however you want and then test it out! Look through the paper towel roll and focus in on different objects.

Extension Idea

This telescope is a great tool for helping us "see" things more clearly. While this low-tech project does not make far-away objects look much closer, it does help our eyes to focus on specific objects by blocking out other distractions.

Take your telescope outside and explore your surroundings. Focus on birds in a tree or bugs on the sidewalk. What details do you notice when you are really paying attention?

Related Projects

Scan the QR codes for STEAM Station episodes.

Paper Planes

Helicopters

Nature Hike

Educator Interview:

What has been your #1 STEAM project with your students? Why?

"My 5th graders create a burglar-proof lunch box. They learn about scale drawings, create blueprints, provide feedback, build their lunch boxes, learn about pitching ideas, and then pitch their idea to the class. I do this as a collaborative project in groups of three and every year, all the kids get super into it."

Heather Laurent

"I truly enjoy creating Rube Goldberg machines with my students. It is so fun seeing them build their chain reactions using whatever materials they have available. Students really get creative when it comes to supplies for this project!"

Rachael Ragan

"One of my favorite activities was when I gave students a design challenge to create an 18-hole miniature golf course. There was so much research about how golf courses are designed, and student-led discussions took place prior to the start of the hands-on making part of this project. Students used low-cost materials such as painter's tape and paper towel rolls to create challenging holes. The 'golf ball' was a Sphero (robot) that they coded to successfully make a hole-in-one when they were finished with their design!"

Ashli Detweiler

"Once of my favorite STEAM projects was an animated book talk diorama. In this project, students take a scene from their favorite book and create an animated scene from the story using Hummingbird robotics and recycled materials. Students really enjoy this experience because they get to express their creativity as they talk about reading. They learn programming and engineering skills while making an artistic representation of what they learned. The discussions they have within their groups are rich with problem solving strategies and conversations around story elements. It is truly a cross-curricular activity."

Shad Wachter

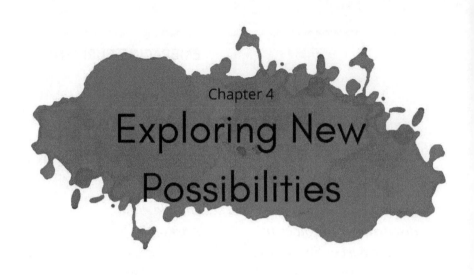

Chapter 4

Exploring New Possibilities

"The goal of education is not to increase the amount of knowledge but to create the possibilities for a child to invent and discover."
Jean Piaget

For science educator **Debbie Reynolds**, STEAM learning has always been a way to engage her learners and help them grow, both as students, and as *people*. "STEAM learning is a way to capture students' interests and help them to discover their passions and strengths," Reynolds explained.

As a Pennsylvania State STEM Ambassador, Reynolds makes it her mission to educate students and other teachers about the important role that STEM fields play in our society. "When I first started teaching, I quickly noticed that a lot of STEM opportunities, or really, a lot of different opportunities in general, were reserved for our Gifted students. That was something I really tried to change in the schools that I have worked in," Reynolds said. "I started providing as many hands-on, real-world learning experiences and field trips to as many students as possible. I've found that when students have these types of experiences, not only are they more engaged in the learning process, but they become more interested in diving deeper and learning more."

Throughout her time in the classroom, Reynolds made connections with local organizations and companies, as well an signed her students up to participate in various competitions. However, Reynolds cautions that educators should not be intimidated if they do not necessarily have connections or funding streams for these opportunities. "The first step is really taking an inventory of students' interests and then exploring how you might make meaningful connections between students' interests and the curriculum. This focus will help you identify possible partners or resources to explore, and you never know who might already have a connection that you could use," Reynolds explained.

Bringing your own passions into the classroom can also help create a sense of "next-level" STEAM learning. "For me, one of my passions is Space. I love everything about it and find that I could organize an entire year-long curriculum around it. When you bring your passion into the classroom, your students can sense your excitement and often, they get excited right along with you," said Reynolds. By introducing her students to her passion for space, Reynolds was then able to tie in math concepts as students calculated the trajectory of a shuttle launch, and biology as student studied the effects of zero gravity on the human body. This also led to side projects focused on aeronautics, environmental implications of growing food in space, and more.

For Reynolds, some of her favorite learning experiences with her students have been ones that have helped them to foster new connections, not only in the

Sciences, but with other students as well. "I do a project called 'Ship the Chip' and it is all about engineering a way to ship a potato chip to a classroom in a different state. Students have to carefully consider materials—not only the physical packaging materials themselves, but also the cost of mailing different types of materials. They have to consider the shipping process—what obstacles might the package face on its journey across the country? Once they create and test their designs, we package the potato chip, send it off, and both classrooms get on a video call to open the packages when they arrive at the school. Students get to see the results of their work, and they also get to meet other students and hear about their design process too," Reynolds explains. (see tryengineering.org for more information)

Reynolds' suggestions for other educators looking to bring more STEAM into the classroom are:

First, take risks. We ask our students to take risks every day, but they need to see us modeling that for them. Recognize that an activity may not go exactly as you planned, but that is okay—the STEAM process is focused on iteration and problem-solving, and as educators, we need to practice that too.

Second, be flexible. Reynolds recommends that teachers "just roll with it" once a project gets started. Allow students to take the reins. Be there to guide students along the way, but have enough flexibility to allow students to pivot, make changes, and create their own discoveries.

Third, frame your STEAM projects around real-world concepts. "I like to start with a book, start with a story, and then end with a creation," said Reynolds. Give students the appropriate background knowledge so that they can make sense of the task, and then provide supports so that students can research, prototype, and gain additional content knowledge.

"Focusing on my passion for space really helped to launch my teaching practices to a new level," reflected

Reynolds. "I would say to any teacher, think about how you can bring your own passions into the classroom and allow those passions to really grow. Allow students to share their passions, too. Many people are already teaching STEM in their classrooms and may not even realize it. You can do it!"

Reynolds' NASA Glove Box project (p. 69) and launcher challenge (p. 85) can be used as inspiration for projects of your own.

Next-Level Design

Reynolds' interest in space helped to elevate her curriculum by providing her with different avenues through which to teach her content. Consider the following questions as you brainstorm ways to bring your own interests into the classroom.

- What is something that I am passionate about that I can share with my students?
- What curriculum topics are related to my area of interest?
- How can I create hands-on learning experiences that help students understand these curriculum topics?
- What connections do I have, or can I make, to outside resources related to these topics that would provide meaningful learning opportunities for my students?

Straw Rockets

Rockets are launched into the air by the force created from their engines. For this experiment, create a miniature rocket of your own that is powered by air.

Scan to access related STEAM Station episode!

Materials:
- Paper
- Straw
- Scissors & Tape

Step #1: Cut a small rectangle of paper about 3 inches by 4 inches and wrap it around your straw.

Step #2: Tape the rolled paper so that is does not come apart, but do not tape it *to* the straw.

Step #3: Using your fingers and tape, close the top of the paper tube by turning it into a cone shape. This is called the *nose cone* and will help your rocket launch into the air.

Step #4: Cut out three or four triangles and tape them to the bottom of your paper tube. These will be the *fins* and they will create stability for the rocket.

Step #5: Add your tube onto the straw and blow into the open end of the straw. Does your rocket launch into the air?

Extension Idea

When you blow into the straw, you create a force that launches the paper rocket into the air. What else can you create that will launch an object?

A catapult is a type of launcher that use potential and kinetic energy. When you pull down on the arm of the catapult and then release it, energy propels whatever is in the bucket forward.

Can you build a catapult?

Space Lander

A space lander is a special spacecraft designed to land on the surface of the moon. Because spacecrafts travel so fast, it is important that a space lander be able to land softly on impact—to protect the vehicle and accomplish its mission. Can you design a space lander that lands safely?

Scan to access related STEAM Station episode!

Materials:
- Paper
- Scissors & Tape
- Recyclables
- Small Toy (as an astronaut!)

Step #1: Your space lander must be able to land on the ground without breaking. Come up with a design that might work to absorb the impact of the fall.

Step #2: At the bottom of your project, think about what you might add to help cushion the landing. Should your space lander have a flat bottom? Springs? Wheels?

Step #3: Create a place on or inside your space lander for your small toy passenger. When you drop the space lander from up high, does it land safely *and* keep the toy in place? If not, what might you change about your design?

Extension Idea

When building a Space Lander, you have to think about how your design will absorb the shock of falling from a great height. Can you challenge yourself to create something else that can land softly?

Design a lander that will help bring something fragile (like an egg!) down to the ground without breaking.
- What types of materials could you use?
- How will you keep the object safe?

Constellations

Constellations are patterns in the stars. When you look at the sky on a clear, dark night, you may be able to see them. Constellations were used in ancient times for navigation, to keep track of time, and to tell stories. Can you create a constellation of your own?

Scan to access related STEAM Station episode!

Materials:
- Paper Tube
- Paper
- Tape
- Safety Pin (to poke holes)
- Flashlight

Step #1: Cut a square of paper that is slightly larger than the opening of your paper tube.

Step #2: On the paper, sketch a simple image (Examples: smiley face or a heart). Then, use your safety pin to carefully poke holes along the lines of your sketch.

Step #3: Tape your paper across the opening on one side of the paper tube.

Step #4: Turn out the lights and shine a flashlight through the other end of your paper tube. Point the image at a blank wall. Can you see your constellation?

Extension Idea

On a clear night, you can see actual constellations in the sky. While some constellations are more visible at certain times of the year, the Big Dipper is one that is often easy to find. The Big Dipper consists of seven bright stars and looks like a bowl with a handle.

Do some research on other constellations and take a look outside. What can you find in the sky?

Data Science

Data Science focuses on gathering information and using that information to look at patterns or make predictions. For this challenge, you will keep track of activities that you do this week and then use that information in a chart.

Scan to access related STEAM Station episode!

Materials:

- Paper
- Markers

Step #1: Keep track of all the new things that you try this week. On a piece of paper, write down the following topics:

- Learned something new
- Ate something new
- Made something new

Step #2: Assign each topic a color by decorating it with your markers.

Step #3: Throughout the week, add more of that color as you do each topic. (For example, each time you eat something new, add a new blue mark to your paper.)

Step #4: At the end of the week, examine your chart. What does it tell you about your week?

Extension Idea

We collect data all the time without even realizing it! In our minds, we keep a list of foods that we like to eat, and a list of foods that we do not like. We keep track of the types and names of our friends' pets. We decide how to dress in the morning based on what we have experienced with the weather.

What other topics can you collect data on today? Survey your friends to find out their favorite sports, keep track of how many times you walk up and down steps, or gather data about the types of books you have on your bookshelf.

Project inspirationt: *Dear Data* by Giorgia Lupi & Stefanie Posavec, 2016

Related Projects

Scan the QR codes for STEAM Station episodes.

NASA Gloves

Masks

Sounds

Educator Interview:

What is something that surprised you about STEAM learning?

"Educators often talk about providing students with 'real-world' learning and problem-solving opportunities. Unfortunately, the talk and the actions don't often align. That's what was so surprising to me about STEAM. When I first began implementing STEAM principles into my instruction, the students quickly began to lose their fear of making mistakes. Additionally, they were able to focus on solutions and not problems. Finally, the students learned that building momentum toward completing a goal is messy, but it is worth it in the end. Failure is the tuition for future success, and STEAM programs provide plenty of opportunities for students to safely learn to manage their emotions regarding success and failure."

Dr. Chuck Herring

71

"When we started STEM a few years ago, we were most surprised that our kids were so used to doing teacher-led activities that they didn't know what to do in an open-ended situation when given a design task. Over the years, the students have improved their confidence, creation skills, curiosity, creativity, and collaboration. Students now work with each other to make improvements on their designs."

Kim Dawson

"The biggest surprise in teaching STEAM is all of the joy and wonder that I get to witness on a daily basis. Students discovering hidden talents and passions brings me such JOY. As a teacher, it is a dream come true to be able to bring these experiences to so many students on a daily basis."

Cari Kelm

Chapter 5

Crafting Solutions

"The innovator's mindset can be defined as the belief that the abilities, intelligence, and talents are developed so that they lead to the creation of new and better ideas."
George Couros

Curriculum Specialist **Mandi Figlioli** strongly believes in project-based learning and its power to improve the school community. "From my ten years of experience in the classroom, I really always believed that hands-on learning was how students learned best," Figlioli explained.

By starting with a grant-funded MakerSpace in her elementary school in 2014 and working with teaching artists from the Children's Museum of Pittsburgh, as well as other local organizations that served as catalysts to help the teachers in her building understand pedagogy, Maker Education strategies, and facilitation of the space, Figoli and her team were able to start the development of Maker culture in her school.

"At first, Making took place strictly in that space, but as teachers started to feel more comfortable, we started to see a lot more Making taking place in the regular classroom too. Co-learning was really a big part of that," said Figlioli.

So often, we think of the teachers as being the ones with the most knowledge in the classroom, but in a co-learning situation—in a *Making* situation—Figlioli focuses on the value of shared experiences and the sharing of knowledge among everyone—Administrators learning alongside teachers, and teachers learning alongside their students. "Creating a community of learners is so important," Figioli explained. "You need a community made up of both outside organizations that can provide support and resources, and a community of people inside your organization who are going to be a driving force for the initiative to really take hold."

Creating a school culture of Making is not something that can happen overnight. Instead, it is important to take the time to build the proper scaffolds so that all stakeholders can find their footing. "Encouraging teachers to bring creativity into the classroom needs to be done by providing teachers with enough time to experience it for themselves first. It starts with meaningful learning experiences for teachers, and those experiences have to simulate what they are going to be doing in the classroom," said Figlioli.

"I think teachers, at heart, really value creativity because we bring so much creativity to our teaching every day. However, there is so much pressure to meet the learning standards and prepare our students for tests. Teachers need the chance to see that Making is equally important. Teachers need to know that it is okay to take risks, and possibly fail.

Teachers need to know that this process can and will take time," Figlioli said.

When reflecting on the positive changes Figlioli sees in students with this shift toward more maker-centered learning, one word comes to mind: JOY. "Not that I think there can't be joy without creative, hands-on projects, but when you see students actively engaged and being in charge of their own learning, there is just so much joy in the classroom. The classroom is noisy, it is full of excitement, and that is what I love to see. The skills students develop when they are in charge of their learning have so much transferability into adulthood. You see students start to gain self-confidence, discover what they are good at, and challenge themselves to learn more, not necessarily for a grade, but because they are intrinsically motivated to dive in," Figlioli explained.

Getting started with hands-on STEAM projects may seem daunting at first, but Figlioli has a few suggestions to help organize and facilitate these experiences:

First, figure out your objective. As a curriculum specialist, Figlioli often looks for organic connections to the curriculum. However, a project does not necessarily need to match up to a specific standard or subject area. Sometimes, you might find it most fitting to design a project based on a current event or a topic of special interest to your students.

Second, take the time to teach your students about the Engineering Design Process. Teach them to ask questions, make blueprints, test their ideas, and iterate on their designs. Additionally, teach them how to use the available materials. Sometimes, students may be overwhelmed by the objects in front of them and may need to be explicitly shown how to cut cardboard, how to make a sturdy base for their project, or how to transfer their ideas from paper into a three-dimensional prototype.

At the core of Making and creativity in the classroom, Figlioli holds *empathy* as a crucial component: "Above all else, we don't just want our students to solve problems that we pose to them, but we want them to *find* problems out in the real world and figure out solutions in order to make the world a better place for others. Cultivating that in the classroom through Making might take some time, but it is so important for our students."

Figlioli's invention challenge is located on page 77.

Engineering Design Process

Figlioli recommends the Engineering Design Process as a framework for helping students work through any design challenge. By encouraging students to ask questions and really understand the problem posed to them, and then brainstorming possible solutions before prototyping, students can learn to make intentional design choices and iterate on their ideas.

Improve   Ask

Create   Imagine

Plan

Inventions

An invention is something new that has not been created before. Have you ever come up with an idea and thought, "That would be really helpful!" or, "That would solve a problem!"? If so, you are ready to be an inventor!

Scan to access related STEAM Station episode!

Materials:
- Craft Supplies
- Recyclables
- Tape and/or Glue

Step #1: Think of a problem that you would like to solve. What could you *build* that would make your problem better?

Step #2: Examine your supplies. How might your use your supplies to build a solution to your problem?

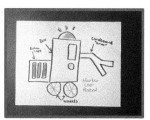

Step #3: Build your idea. Make sure to add plenty of detail and test it out to see if your solution works.

Step #4: Improve your design by getting feedback from others and incorporating their suggestions into your project. Test your invention out again!

Extension Idea

Part of being a strong designer is knowing *who* you are designing an invention for. Before coming up with a project idea, spend some time interviewing someone about a problem they face or about one of their needs. This *empathy interview* can help to provide a greater purpose for your invention.

Marble Maze

Creating a marble maze not only requires problem-solving skills, but also hand-eye coordination! Can you create a path for your marble to roll from the beginning to the end while navigating obstacles and possible traps?

Scan to access related STEAM Station episode!

Materials:
- Paper Plate
- Paper
- Scissors & Glue
- Marble

Step #1: On your paper plate, label the Start and End of your maze. Cut a hole near the endpoint so that your marble can fit through.

Step #2: Cut multiple strips of paper. Paper strips should be about ½ inch wide by 4 inches long. Fold the edges of each strip to create two tabs. This is where the glue will go.

Step #3: Glue each tab to the plate to create a course for your marble maze. You may want to draw arrows to show where the marble should travel.

Step #4: Add your marble and test out your course. Gently move the plate around to navigate the marble through the strips. Can you make it to the end?

Extension Idea

Use this activity as an "unplugged" low-tech programming activity by first writing the sequence of directions that the marble must travel to make it through the maze.

Looking for an additional challenge? Increase the size and difficulty of the maze by creating a course using Legos, building blocks, or other materials!

Chain Reaction

A chain reaction is when one thing happens because of something else. It is the perfect design challenge for exploring *Cause and Effect*! Can you build a chain reaction display that will make something happen?

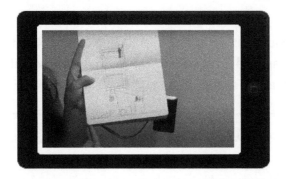

Scan to access related
STEAM Station episode!

Materials:
- Found Objects
- String
- Craft Supplies
- Recyclables

Step #1: Examine the supplies that you have available to you. How could you use them in a chain reaction design?

Step #2: Draw out a plan. What task will your Chain Reaction design be able to accomplish? Will it roll a ball into a cup? Knock down a book?

Step #3: Begin building. Test each step as you go to make sure each aspect of your chain reaction works as it should.

Step #4: Refine your design until your chain reaction is able to accomplish its task.

Extension Idea

Use this project as an opportunity to investigate *Rube Goldberg*— an inventor, engineer, and cartoonist who was known for creating elaborate chain reactions to accomplish simple tasks. Using his projects as inspiration, can you add elements of simple machines to your chain reaction design?

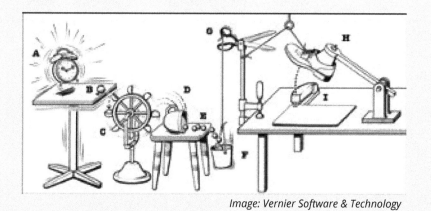

Image: Vernier Software & Technology

Building Design

Inspiration for new creations is all around us! Simple materials can be used to create *prototypes*—models of what creations would look like if they were real. For this challenge, gain inspiration from buildings around you to create a structure using recycled materials.

Scan to access related STEAM Station episode!

Materials:

- Recyclables
- Cardboard
- Tape
- Craft Materials (optional)
- Paint (optional)

Step #1: Decide on the type of building that you want to create. Is it tall like a skyscraper? Detailed like a castle? Long and low like a stadium?

Step #2: Gather recycled materials that remind you of the type of structure you plan to create. For example, if making a castle, can you find something shaped like a turret (the curved, pointed objects on a castle)?

Step #3: Build your structure using your recycled materials and tape. As you build, consider what details you could add, like paint or craft supplies, to improve your building design.

Extension Idea

Use this project as an opportunity to focus on the importance of blueprints to the design process. Blueprints are technical drawings that focus specifically on the supplies and measurements needed to create a structure.

By creating detailed blueprints, you gain a deeper understanding of the supplies needed for your design, as well as how much space your project will require. For this project, challenge yourself to spend more time than usual in the planning phase of the design process and see how it impacts your final product.

Related Projects

Scan the QR codes for STEAM Station episodes.

Chair Design

Launcher

Educator Interview:

What is your best tip for organizing materials or facilitating low-tech STEAM projects?

"Organizing materials can be tricky. It's worth investing in extra shelving if you do not have a lot of cabinet space. I highly recommend shelving that can be moved around your room. The ability to move things from place to place is priceless."

Aaron Colf

"I use the lockers outside one of my classrooms to organize. The Office put the spare lockers near me to give me this luxury. When planning a last-minute project (within a couple weeks), ask different classrooms in the school to collect different items (for example, paper towel rolls, egg cartons, etc.)."

Colleen Hinrichsen

"Store materials in bins. They can be easily transported to any place you need them and readily available for students to help with cleanup. Provide necessary group materials in the center of each table (such as, scissors, glue sticks, tape, etc.)."

Jody Kokladas

"My best tip for organizing supplies would be to take whatever space you have and organize it into zones. For example: MakerSpace, Robotics, Circuitry, Videography etc. Then keep supplies in corresponding zones that would typically be used during activities."

Cari Kelm

Continuing Creatively

Aileen Owens

Director & Consultant, ThroughlinesEdu

No doubt this book has been an inspiration for many; a chance to learn, test new ideas, and to imagine the possibilities. It may be your first experience engaging in the creative process, or it may be a time to reconnect with ideas in a new way. What matters is that you do not stop here. Use this experience as a springboard to pursue your creative passion and develop confidence as a Maker. As educators and as parents, we want to help our children grow as creative problem-solvers and find meaningful careers where they can thrive. How can we guide them when we may not feel confident in our own abilities?

Experts explain that creativity is a mindset; a problem-solving process we can develop. We know that we are most creative when we find things we are passionate about. Entrepreneurial ideas and innovative design are fueled by inspiration. We can encourage our children to continue growing their creative spirit by seeking new opportunities. Inspiration happens with exploration. We can encourage our children to pursue activities and experiences that spark their imagination and ignite their passion as they gain a deeper understanding of who they are along the way.

These concepts seem vague, until you can see them through someone else's experience.

Aditi Srivastava, a rising high school senior, is host to a podcast called Inter*gal*actic which is supported through the Astrobotic Foundation and found on Apple podcasts. Aditi hosts interviews with inspiring women in space, technology, and beyond to illuminate new perspectives on the future of space. In a recent interview with Stella Guillen, Vice President of Sales and Marketing at Arianespace, Stella spoke about what it is like to be a woman coming up in the space technology industry. She came to the United States from Latin America as a professional ballet dancer in her early twenties and worked in sales on the side. She explained that ballet was her passion and nothing else. That is until one day, she stumbled into a building for a job interview and in the lobby she saw satellite mockups hanging from the ceiling. The manager showed her a video about the company. It happened to be a consortium of governments founded under a resolution from the United Nations to establish that communication by means of satellite should be available for all nations. Stella said it was at that moment that she fell in love with the idea of satellites connecting people all over the world; the human purpose behind the technology. She pushed herself to learn. She took all the courses you could possibly take, and this ballet dancer found her way into an industry led predominately by engineers.

Her advice for every student is to be open to new opportunities—they come unexpectedly in different ways. Stella reminds us to be open to the changes you experience and recognize how you feel, especially to be honest with yourself. She encourages us to continue to explore and gain knowledge. If you are passionate about space, do not limit yourself to technology and science. For instance, fashion designers are now involved in the design of spacesuits. A photographer must think about photos in a different way because of the way pictures are captured in space. We may soon have construction jobs in space as the possibility of space tourism advances. The career opportunities are endless—medicine, life science, astrobiology—they are all related to space exploration.

My hope is that this book will be the beginning of the creative courage you find to pursue your passion and make a difference in your world. Within each new exploration, there will be throughlines that will lead you to your next adventure. Continue to create and follow where it leads. We will be there cheering you on.

About the Authors

 **Melissa Unger:** As an elementary STEAM teacher in the South Fayette School District, Melissa teaches students the beginnings of computer programming and helps them to design, build, and bring their ideas to life as they experiment, invent, and use technology. A life-long maker, Melissa's elementary STEAM curriculum intertwines art and science and challenges students to think critically while using their imaginations to construct new realities. Melissa leads out-of-school computer programming clubs for upper elementary students, family nights for the community, and STEAM professional development for educators. Melissa is also a member of Agency by Design and is currently working on her doctorate in STEM Education.

 **Anna V. Blake:** As a technology integrator, Anna teaches over 400 children each year the fundamentals of computational thinking and computer science to grades K through 5 in the Elizabeth Forward School District. She has presented at both local and international conferences about computational thinking and Making in an elementary school setting. She also sits on the Duquesne University Alumni Advisory Board and volunteers her time to help pre-service teachers prepare for their time in the classroom. In her free time, she enjoys reading, scrapbooking, and traveling.

CPSIA information can be obtained
at www.ICGtesting.com
Printed in the USA
LVHW082012090222
710662LV00003B/33

9 781387 260577